THE ROSWELL UFO INCIDENT

By Blake Hoena
Illustration By Tate Yotter
Color By Gerardo Sandoval

BELLWETHER MEDIA • MINNEAPOLIS, MN

Stray from regular reads with Black Sheep books. Feel a rush with every read!

Library of Congress Cataloging-in-Publication Data

Names: Hoena, B. A., author.
Title: The Roswell UFO Incident / by Blake Hoena.
Description: Minneapolis, MN : Bellwether Media, Inc., 2020. | Series: Black Sheep: Paranormal Mysteries | Includes bibliographical references and index. | Audience: Grade: 3 to 7. |
Identifiers: LCCN 2019003758 (print) | LCCN 2019005385 (ebook) | ISBN 9781618916693 (ebook) | ISBN 9781644870976 (hardcover : alk. paper) | ISBN 9781618917355 (pbk. : alk. paper)
Subjects: LCSH: Unidentified flying objects–Sightings and encounters–New Mexico–Roswell Region–Juvenile literature.
Classification: LCC TL789.5.N6 (ebook) | LCC TL789.5.N6 H64 2020 (print) | DDC 001.94209789/43–dc23
LC record available at https://lccn.loc.gov/2019003758

This edition first published in 2020 by Bellwether Media, Inc.

Editor: Christina Leaf Designer: Andrea Schneider

Printed in the United States of America, North Mankato, MN.

Table of Contents

Red text identifies historical quotes.

The Flying Saucer Craze

Newspapers offered rewards for proof that UFOs existed. But some people thought they were a joke.
Be on the lookout for flying saucers up there.
Ha! And don't forget the little green men.
I'll believe them when I see them.
July 4, 1947:
Captain E.J. Smith was aboard United Air Lines flight 105.
Captain, what are those?
I can't believe it. They must be flying saucers.
Smith, co-pilot Ralph Stevens, and flight attendant Marty Morrow all claimed to have seen several flying saucers.
Marty, can you up come up here?
It's those flying saucers!
But the most famous UFO incident was about to occur days later.

The Roswell Incident

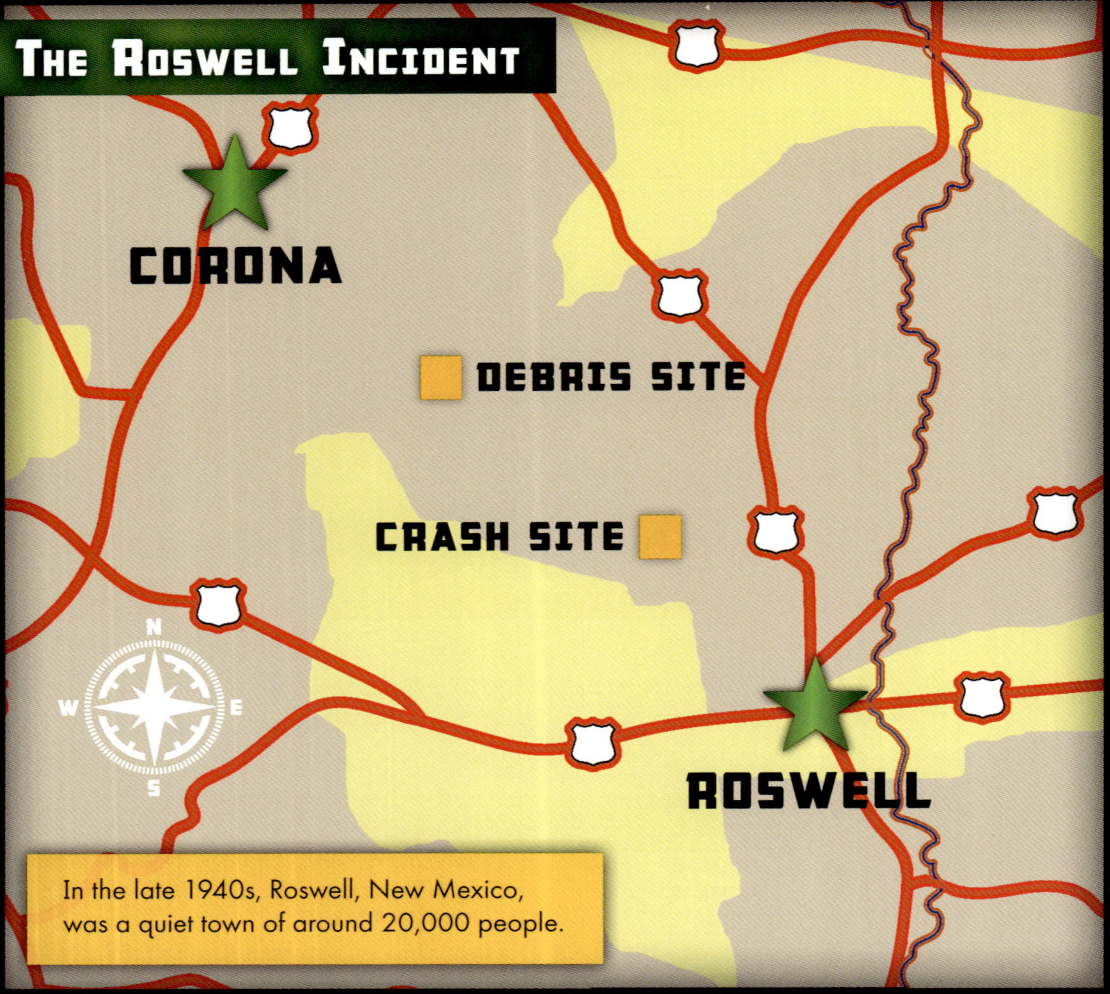

In the late 1940s, Roswell, New Mexico, was a quiet town of around 20,000 people.

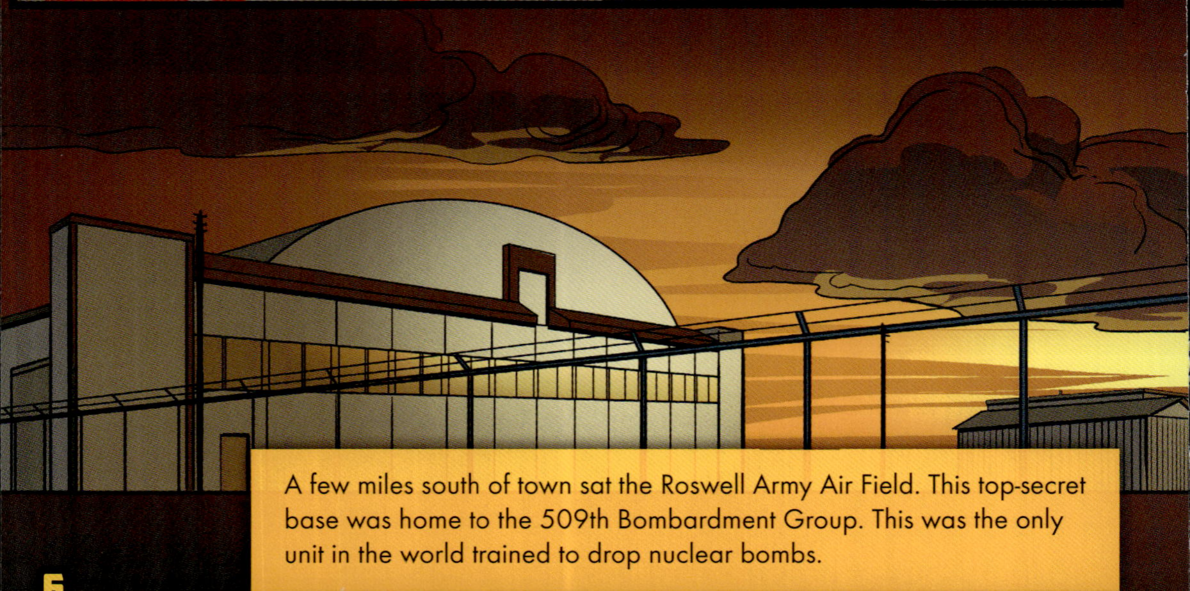

A few miles south of town sat the Roswell Army Air Field. This top-secret base was home to the 509th Bombardment Group. This was the only unit in the world trained to drop nuclear bombs.

July 2, 1947:
Dan and Mary Wilmot were sitting on the front porch of their home in Roswell.
Do you see that, dear? What is it?
I don't know. Let's get a better look.
It's flying pretty fast.
I bet 500 miles an hour or so.
Should we tell anyone?
It might be best to keep this to ourselves. Let someone else report it.

The Wilmots were not the only ones to see something strange. Mac Brazel lived and worked on J.B. Foster's ranch, not far from Roswell. A few weeks earlier, he was waiting out a storm.
Hope this storm doesn't cause too much damage.
The day after the storm blew through the area, Brazel went to check on things around the ranch.
What's wrong with those sheep?
They want nothing to do with this **debris**.

Strange. I've never seen anything like this.
July 7, 1947: On a trip into town, Brazel showed Sheriff Wilcox what he found.
Could it be from one of those flying saucers the newspapers keep talking about?
I'm not sure.
But whatever it is, I'm going to let the folks over at the base know about it.

Later that day, Air Force Major Jesse Marcel met with Brazel.
You say you found this out on the Foster ranch?
Yeah, about 70 miles from here. I can take you out there.
It's spread out there, over a couple hundred feet.
Have you seen anything like this before?
Never. Some of it looks as if it's not from this world.
I'll drive it all back to base.
01168

On his way to the base, **rumors** say that Marcel stopped at his home. He wanted to show his family what had been found.
What's all this?
Debris I picked up out on the Foster ranch.
Wow! Where did this come from?
I don't know. Maybe outer space.

Marcel had the debris taken to the Roswell air base. It was then flown to Fort Worth Army Air Base. There, Brigadier General Roger Ramey examined it.
What do you make of it, General?
This foil is some of the strangest material I've ever seen.
July 8, 1947:
The Roswell air base issued a **press release** about the debris from the Foster ranch.
...the Army Air Forces has announced that a flying disk has been found and is now in the possession of the Army...
By this time, the Wilmots had mentioned what they saw flying through the sky. Their story was part of an article printed in local papers.
It says you heard swishing sounds as it flew overhead.
I did, just for a few seconds.

But that same day, Ramey took back the earlier press release.
Is it true that a flying saucer was found?
Reports of a flying disk crashing in the desert near Roswell are false. No evidence of flying saucers was found.
What was found was a crashed weather balloon. Check for yourselves.
That's a radar reflector. It is used to track the balloon's position.
What is this strange foil then?
For the next 30 years, all but a few people believed Ramey's story.

Rumors and Witnesses

Over time, other stories surfaced as researchers **investigated** events near Roswell in 1947. One involved Grady "Barney" Barnett. He was working near Socorro, New Mexico, about 150 miles from Roswell. One day while driving, he saw something shocking.

Before Barnett could get a better look at the body, the United States military swooped in.
Sir, this area is off-limits to **civilians**. You must leave at once.
You will speak of this to no one, is that clear?
No one would believe me if I did.
Barnett died in 1969. Before he did, he had shared with friends and family what he had seen. They told his story.

Another story centers around Glenn Dennis. He was a **mortician** working at a funeral home in Roswell. One afternoon, he received a strange call from the Army Air Field hospital.
Do you have any child-sized coffins?
I'm pretty sure I can find some.
Later that evening, Dennis drove over to the base.
I wonder what that wreckage is from.
Dennis entered the hospital, thinking his help might be needed.
EXIT
Are there any bodies from the crash...?
Get this guy off the base. He's not supposed to be here.
As he was being led out of the hospital, Dennis saw a nurse he knew.
Glenn, get out of here as fast as you can!
What's going on?
AUTHORIZED PERSONNEL ONLY

The next morning, Dennis met with the nurse.
What was that wreckage from?
A flying saucer. Several alien bodies were found.
They looked something like this.

Dennis never saw the nurse again after that day. She was moved to a different base. He did not tell his story until years later.

Roswell Today

For years, rumors continued about flying saucers in Roswell. In response, the U.S. Army chose to **declassify** documents related to the event. In 1994, information about Project Mogul was released. This secret program from the late 1940s used large weather balloons.

A trail of radar reflectors hung from the balloons. They were made of the same material that Brazel found on the Foster ranch.

The balloons also carried microphones and **sensors**. The U.S. Army hoped these could detect enemy nuclear bomb tests.

In 1997, information about Operation High Dive was released. This secret program from the 1950s tested **high-altitude** parachutes. Dummies were lifted into the air and then dropped to the ground.
Usually the military collected the dummies right after they crashed. But in some cases, people found them first. It is believed that these **mangled** dummies were mistaken for aliens.

It has been more than 70 years since Brazel found the strange debris on Foster's ranch. In that time, Roswell has grown into a city of nearly 50,000 people.
UFO MUSEUM
Roswell is now a popular travel spot. Many consider it the UFO capital of the world. People from around the world visit every year for the UFO Festival. There are parades.
In my book, *Crash at Corona*, I go into detail about why I believe Barney Barnett's story.
Famous UFO investigators give talks. They speak about evidence that they have found.
Do you really think they found aliens?
Some people say they did.
People visit the Roswell UFO Museum.
I bet there are space aliens out there somewhere.
There are film showings, bands, planetarium shows, and much more.

UFO
MUSEUM
AND
RESEARCH
CENTER
UFO MUSEUM
Could a weather balloon have inspired all of this?
I doubt it.
The U.S. military says the question of Roswell is done. But people still believe in stories of flying saucers crashing somewhere in the deserts of New Mexico. The mystery of Roswell lingers...

Theories Behind the Incident

- Most of what is known about the Roswell incident comes from secondhand stories. People claim to have known someone who witnessed events, like Barnett. Barnett never recorded what he saw. Rather, his story has been told by family and friends. Over time, details often get changed as stories are retold. This makes them difficult to trust.
- Dennis claimed that a nurse friend told him of the alien bodies. He did not see them, and the identity of the nurse is unknown. It cannot be proven that she saw what Dennis says she witnessed, or that the nurse even existed.
- Project High Dive began in the early 1950s. The U.S. Army claims it is the cause for humanlike alien figures being found in the desert. But the events surrounding the Roswell incident occurred years earlier.
- Several UFO investigators believe that the debris Brazel found was switched. When Ramey held his press conference, they say the original debris was replaced with materials from a weather balloon.

Timeline

July 2, 1947: Mr. and Mrs. Wilmot claim to see a strange, glowing, saucer-like craft fly overhead

July 7, 1947: Mac Brazel heads into Roswell to show Sheriff Wilcox some unusual debris he found

July 8, 1947: A press release says that the U.S. Army found a flying saucer, but Brigadier General Roger Ramey holds a press conference later, stating that the debris was a weather balloon

July 9, 1947: The military rejects claims that a flying saucer was found with a second press release

Glossary

civilians—people who are not members of the military or part of the police and firefighting services

Cold War—a conflict between the United States and the former Soviet Union in the second half of the 20th century

debris—the scattered pieces of something broken down or destroyed

declassify—to make formerly secret information public

evidence—facts and materials that prove whether or not something is true

high-altitude—high up in the sky

investigated—searched for facts

mangled—badly injured from tearing or crushing

mortician—a person who prepares bodies for burial or cremation

nuclear bombs—extremely powerful explosive devices that use nuclear reactions

press release—an official statement given to a newspaper or news organization

radar reflector—something that is made to reflect radio waves, which make it visible on radar devices

rumors—talk with no clear source or truth

sensors—devices that respond to light, pressure, sound, or other physical changes

UFO—unidentified flying object; UFOs are often thought to be alien spacecraft, although any unknown flying object can be called a UFO.

To Learn More

AT THE LIBRARY

Hile, Lori. *Aliens and UFOs: Myth or Reality?* North Mankato, Minn.: Capstone Press, 2019.

Loh-Hagan, Virginia. *Roswell.* Ann Arbor, Mich.: Cherry Lake Publishing, 2018.

Oachs, Emily Rose. *UFOs*. Minneapolis, Minn.: Bellwether Media, 2019.

ON THE WEB

FACTSURFER

Factsurfer.com gives you a safe, fun way to find more information.

1. Go to www.factsurfer.com
2. Enter "Roswell UFO incident" into the search box and click 🔍.
3. Select your book cover to see a list of related web sites.

Index